W9-CFI-678

Death of an Empire

The Prophetic Destiny
of the Soviet Union

Death of an Empire

The Prophetic Destiny
of the Soviet Union

by
Dr. Hilton Sutton

Harrison House
Tulsa, Oklahoma

Unless otherwise indicated, all Scripture quotations are taken from the *King James Version* of the Bible.

Scripture quotations marked NIV are taken from *The Holy Bible: New International Version.* Copyright © 1973, 1978, 1984 by the International Bible Society. Used by permission of Zondervan Bible Publishers.

Scripture quotations marked NKJV are taken from *The New King James Version* of the Bible. Copyright © 1979, 1980, 1982 by Thomas Nelson, Inc., Publishers. Used by permission.

Death of an Empire —
The Prophetic Destiny of the Soviet Union
ISBN 0-89274-882-6
Copyright © 1991 by Hilton Sutton
Hilton Sutton Ministries
736 Wilson Road
Humble, Texas 77338

Published by Harrison House, Inc.
P. O. Box 35035
Tulsa, Oklahoma 74153

Printed in the United States of America. All rights reserved under International Copyright Law. Contents and/or cover may not be reproduced in whole or in part in any form without the express written consent of the Publisher.

Contents

Death of an Empire

The Prophetic Destiny
of the Soviet Union

Introduction

1989 and 1990 were, without question, two very unusual years. I'm certain that each of us can think of major events which have occurred during our lifetime — events of tremendous importance, perhaps even affecting us directly.

But thinking back, I can't recall — in my lifetime, or even that of my parents' — years as momentous, important, dynamic, and unusual as '89 and '90. It seems the order for those years was CHANGE.

God is using many of the events in our world, at this time, to bring about unquestionable changes — changes no one even dreamed of just a short time ago. In fact, many people would not have believed that recent world changes could have occurred in their lifetime.

Could it be that, through all of these unusual events, God is attempting to get the attention of the Church? I am convinced that change is also necessary for those of us who make up the Church.

God speaks through the Apostle Paul in Hebrews 10:19-25. I recommend that you study the whole chapter, but particularly verses 19-25. **And let us consider one another to provoke unto love and to good works** (v. 24). The *New King James Version* says, **And let us consider one another in order to stir up love and good works.** The word "consider," as used in this text, means "to keep each other in mind or to have regard for one another." Surely we care enough about each other to follow biblical instructions for one another's spiritual welfare.

We have a godly responsibility concerning our walk in the love of God and godly works. Remember, by our love for one another, it becomes evident that God dwells in us (see 1 John 4:12). Works are extremely important. Jesus declares in John 14:12 that we are responsible for carrying on His work and Revelation 2:23 reveals that we are rewarded according to our works.

Verse 25 continues, **Not forsaking the assembling of ourselves together, as the manner of some is.** What a powerful statement. Paul points out there will be some Christians who will ignore this divine biblical instruction. **But exhorting one another:** (encouraging one another to love and good works) **and so much the more, as ye see the day approaching.** We are to encourage and motivate each other to be obedient to the Word. We are to stir each other up to love and good works. This is a normal relationship between believers.

The "day" referred to here is the day of the glorious appearing of our Lord and Savior Jesus Christ.

You may ask, "How do you know that?" Let me direct you to Romans 13:11, **And that, knowing the time, that now it is high time to awake out of sleep: for now is our salvation nearer than when we believed.** The salvation Paul refers to is the final phase of the plan of salvation which occurs at Christ's second appearing. God is speaking to those who have already believed and been washed in His blood. He is referring to a phase of salvation they do not as yet have. It is the same phase Jesus mentions in Luke 21:28, **Look up, and lift up your heads; for your redemption draweth nigh.** It is the same phase of salvation that Paul refers to in 1 Corinthians 15:51-53 and Hebrews 9:28.

He speaks concerning those who are looking for the appearing of Jesus, at which time their redemption will be completed. John assists us with the understanding in 1 John 3:2, **Beloved, now are we the sons of God, and it doth not**

yet appear what we shall be: but we know that, when he shall appear, we shall be like him; for we shall see him as he is. So we know that, at the glorious appearing of our Lord for the express purpose of receiving a glorious Church unto Himself, the final phase of salvation will take place for those who have already believed.

This act of redemption is the glorification of the physical body. Our spirits have already been recreated and our souls have been washed in Jesus' blood. Our minds have been transformed by the power of God. But our physical bodies have not yet been glorified. They will not be glorified until the Lord appears in the heavens to await the coming up of His glorious Church.

At that time, the final phase of salvation of the plan of redemption takes place. The glorification of our physical bodies causes the believers to then be exactly like Him in whom they have believed.

Paul states in Hebrews 10:25 that as we see that day of the Lord's appearing approaching, we ought to be motivating and encouraging each other, in order to stir up love and good works. We should be assembling ourselves with one another more and more, as we see the day of the Lord approaching.

1
God is Having His Way

How do we know the Day of the Lord is approaching? We know that because we are seeing the fulfillment of the prophecies of God's Word almost daily. Prophecies make up more than one-third of the contents of the Bible and they are important indicators to us.

The first prophecy is found in Genesis 3:15. **And I will put enmity between thee and the woman, and between thy seed and her seed; it shall bruise thy head, and thou shalt bruise his heel.** There God prophesied to Satan that the seed of the woman he had just deceived was going to bruise his head. The seed of the woman was Jesus Christ. Four thousand years passed before that prophecy was fulfilled. But the prophecy was fulfilled! Satan's head was bruised permanently. He discovered that what God prophesies does come to pass. That's one of the reasons Satan hates Bible prophecy and does his utmost to keep God's people from studying and understanding it. He particularly hates the Book of Revelation because it reveals Jesus' destruction of Satan's best plan and Satan's end in the lake of fire. He would rather you not know about that.

A consistent study of the prophecies in the Scripture reveals the coming glorious event of the appearing of our Lord Jesus Christ. His appearing is as much a prophesied event as was the bruising of Satan's head, which we know was fulfilled. Multitudes of prophecies have been fulfilled throughout the ages and today we have more prophecies being fulfilled than ever before. When we see prophecies being fulfilled which set the stage for the glorious appearance of Jesus Christ to receive His glorious Church unto Himself, we know it is also the moment when we will be changed, in the twinkling of an eye — corruption putting on incorruption and mortality, immortality (see 1 Cor. 15:51-53).

A Time for Change

The months of November and December 1989 were certainly times packed with the fulfillment of Bible prophecies. It is evident that God is calling for a change — a change in world affairs and a change in the Church. Every believer should strive to be more like Jesus now more than ever before.

Hebrews 10:24,25 and Romans 13:11 describe only part of the change that must take place in us. I am convinced that the Holy Spirit is going to get our attention in one way or another. It is now vitally important that we study God's Word and become obedient. We must allow the Holy Spirit to guide us into all truth and direct our steps.

At the onset of 1989, we were aware that Mikhail Gorbachev, leader of the Soviet Union, had introduced perestroika and glasnost. Perestroika simply means "reform or change" — reform for the Soviet Union and the nations over which it has control. Glasnost, "openness," allows the Soviet Union, and the nations controlled by them, to be open to the rest of the world. Therefore, the tearing down of the Iron Curtain and the Berlin Wall is evidence that God is having His way. He is using Gorbachev just as He used Pharaoh.

One might ask, "Does Mr. Gorbachev know that what he is doing is because God is having His way?" He has not brought about reform and openness in order to please God. He has done so because of the great pressure on his government and against international communism by the people of the Soviet Union. Eastern European nations and China are also under great pressure to reform.

Gorbachev has been left with no alternative but to bring about reform and openness. As we proceed, it will become all the more evident that God is having His way and tremendous changes are taking place.

The Origin of Communism

The Iron Curtain, which shut off the Soviet Union from the rest of the world, was the result of the Communist Revolution that began in 1917, during World War I. By the end of the war, in 1918, that revolution had completed its first phase and Lenin was in power.

The philosophy of communism was the product of Karl Marx, but Vladimir Lenin was the architect. Lenin was followed by Joseph Stalin. Their hands were bloody as they executed millions of Russians and people of other Soviet republics who either resisted their takeover or were dedicated to Jesus Christ.

So the Iron Curtain actually began to exist during World War I, 1917, 1918, and was enlarged by Stalin. Stalin forcibly annexed fourteen neighboring republics to Russia, creating the Soviet Union. After World War II, in 1949, Stalin gained control of eastern Europe — East Germany, Poland, Hungary, Czechoslovakia, Romania, and Bulgaria.

In 1949, the "big three" met together — Churchill of England, Truman of the United States, and Joseph Stalin. When their deliberations ended, East Germany, Poland, Hungary, Czechoslovakia, Romania, and Bulgaria had been turned over to the Soviet Union. The Warsaw Pact Treaty, a military alliance controlled by the Soviet Union, then came into existence.

In the same year, 1949, the government of China, under General Chiang Kai-shek, was overthrown by Mao Tse-tung and Chou En-lai. Leading communist armies, these two men defeated General Chiang Kai-shek and took over the government of China. Chiang's government was forced into exile on the island of Formosa, known also as Taiwan. Chairman Mao created the Bamboo Curtain of China.

The Berlin Wall came about in August, 1961, dividing East Berlin from West Berlin. The wall was almost an impregnable barrier, preventing anyone from going from one area to the other. As we know, the Berlin Wall came tumbling down in November, 1989. The year 1989 also witnessed the fall of the Iron Curtain. The Bamboo Curtain of China was ripped from top to bottom, but still remains partially closed at this writing.

A More Sure Word

To understand these prophesied events one must study the prophetic scriptures. There are seventeen prophetic books; sixteen in the Old Testament, Isaiah through Malachi; and Revelation in the New Testament. There are many prophetic statements throughout God's Word, beginning in Genesis 3:15.

As you study the Bible, you will find numerous places where God prophesied. He often prophesied through the psalmists. He prophesied through Jesus Christ in the Gospels. He prophesied through Paul and Peter in their Epistles, as well as in seventeen other prophetic books of the Word of God.

We have also a more sure word of prophecy: ...**whereunto ye do well that ye take heed, as unto a light that shineth in a dark place, until the day dawn, and the day star arise in your hearts** (2 Pet. 1:19). Jesus Christ is the Morning Star. He brings the light of life into our hearts. His birth, ministry, death, and resurrection cast a greater light of understanding on the prophetic books. When prophecies are fulfilled, the prophetic Word is made more sure.

Peter continues in verse 20, **Knowing this first, that no prophecy of the scripture is of any private interpretation.** No one has the right to privately interpret prophecy. Some will say, "How, then, is it to be interpreted?" It is to be taken literally, as the Word of God. It doesn't need to be interpreted. When one studies the Word of God carefully, inviting the help of the Holy Spirit, the Word of God will speak for Itself and interpret Itself. It does not require human interpretation.

That's one of the problems we have had for centuries — men and women trying to interpret the Word of God and not letting It speak for Itself. God said what He wanted to say and He said it very clearly. The Word of God should always be taken literally. Only when figures of speech are used, indicating a symbol, is the Scripture to be so interpreted. An example of such symbolism appears in Daniel with the references to Satan as a roaring lion. However, one notices the literal true message is not changed.

Verse 21 continues, **For the prophecy came not in old time by the will of man: but holy men of God spake as they were moved by the Holy Ghost.** How interesting. We are about to address prophecies that coincide and are harmonious with perestroika, glasnost, and the events of November 1989. We have received some good insight from the Apostle Peter concerning prophecy. As God continues to have His way, prophecies will rapidly be fulfilled.

Prophecies have come to us from God through the Holy Spirit. As prophecies are being fulfilled, they set the stage for additional prophetic fulfillment. Of the prophecies yet to be fulfilled, there are those which describe the glorious appearing of our Lord to receive unto Himself a Church which is mature, successful, productive, and ready. The events of Christ's appearing are hastening upon us as Bible prophecies are being fulfilled more rapidly than ever before.

"It Shall Come to Pass"

Now let us examine the harmony of world affairs and the prophecies of the Scripture. From Isaiah 2:2 an interesting event is prophesied. **And it shall come to pass in the last days, that the mountain of the Lord's house shall be established in the top of the mountains, and shall be exalted above the hills; and all nations shall flow unto it.** Notice the word choice in verse 2. The prophet says, **And it shall come to pass.** Whenever the prophet of God, under the anointing of the Holy Ghost, declares, ''It shall come to pass,'' whatever follows is as certain to occur as the rising and setting of the sun. The prophesied event will absolutely come to pass, because it is a prophecy of the Scripture.

Please notice, the words of the New Testament prophet and those given through the gift of prophecy must be judged! The Apostle Paul makes it very clear in First Corinthians 2:15 that if we are spiritual, we will judge all things. **But He that is spiritual judgeth all things, yet He Himself is judged of no man.** Every prophetic utterance, dream, vision, and revelation must be judged before anyone takes it to heart and acts on it. Paul exhorts us to **Prove all things; hold fast that which is good** (1 Thess. 5:21). We also are to **try the spirits whether they are of God** (1 John 4:1).

There is certainly a difference in the work of the prophet in the Old Testament and the work of the prophet in the New Testament. Today, when a man of God uses the statement, ''It shall come to pass,'' he assumes great responsibility for what he is saying. If, by chance, what is spoken does not come to pass, God says He had nothing to do with it. Therefore, the man who spoke is a false prophet, one who prophesies out of his own spirit.

The Prophet Isaiah prophesied more than 2,600 years ago and said, It shall come to pass in the latter days, which is the same as the last days. The Church has now witnessed more than 1,900 years of ''last days,'' which began with the ministry of Jesus Christ. It is impossible to accurately pinpoint the exact day when the "last days" began.

We do know that the initial outpouring of the Holy Spirit, as recorded in Acts 2, was a last-days event. Isaiah's prophecy is also designated as a last-days event. Let's determine whether or not the prophecy has already come to pass. Isaiah continues the prophecy, **The mountain of the Lord's house shall be established in the top of the mountains, and shall be exalted above the hills; and all nations shall flow into it** (Isa. 2:2).

There is a biblical rule of interpretation concerning the word "mountain." When the word appears in a verse of Scripture and a specific mountain is not identified, either by name or geographical location, then the word "mountain" is being used symbolically. It symbolizes a kingdom. A further examination of the biblical context in which the word is used without identifying an existing mountain, always identifies a kingdom of men.

So it is with the word "hills." "Hills" identify nations, as mountains identify kingdoms. Isaiah declares that nations will flow into the mountain (kingdom) of the Lord's house. This is good news. Nations will flow into God's kingdom in the last days. God will exalt His kingdom over the kingdoms and nations of this world to such a degree that all nations shall flow into it.

That's interesting because we have a fellow prophet who agrees with Isaiah. This Scripture teaches, **In the mouth of two or three witnesses shall every word be established** (2 Cor. 13:1). So, let's go to Micah 4:1: **But in the last days it shall come to pass, that the mountain of the house of the Lord shall be established in the top of the mountains, and it shall be exalted above the hills; and people shall flow into it.**

Isaiah said, nations shall flow into it, and Micah said, people shall flow into it. Again, we apply the rule of biblical interpretation and we understand they are describing kingdoms and nations. People populate and create nations and the prophets declare, All nations shall flow into God's kingdom. It's important to note that Isaiah and Micah are speaking of the same prophetic event.

Who Will Be in God's Kingdom?

Notice the scripture refers to all nations, with no exclusions. Here is the reason the Prophet Isaiah speaks the word "nation" and the Prophet Micah speaks the word "people." Had the word "nations" not been used, there would be teachers and others who would leave out certain nations, saying they were too ungodly or too wicked and had already had their opportunity.

But since Isaiah said **all nations,** there can be no exclusions anywhere on earth, not even the Soviet Union. There can be no exclusion of Muslim nations, African nations, the Orient, European nations, or the nations of the Western hemisphere. There cannot be a single nation left out for any reason, not even the United States.

Thank God for Micah's confirmation of Isaiah's prophecy. People from all nations will flow into God's kingdom because He is exalting it above the kingdoms and nations of this world.

The plan of God is carried out by the Holy Spirit. Here we have two passages of Scripture, given by two individual prophets fifty years apart, who are in absolute agreement with one another. It is a Bible truth that there will come a day in which people from all nations will flow into the kingdom of God. And we, the Church, must recognize this truth.

Until 1989, the Soviet Union controlled fifteen Soviet republics and the eastern European nations. Communism has also controlled China and other oriental nations. Some two billion people of the world's population had been restricted, with freedom of religion withheld from them. It was with great difficulty that the Word of God reached them as Bibles had to be smuggled into their countries.

Prior to perestroika, glasnost, and the closing months of 1989, some two billion of the world's five billion population did not enjoy religious freedom. They were suppressed. For such a massive group of people to be free to flow into the kingdom of God, everything which restricted and enslaved them had to come down. Isaiah and Micah prophesied the coming of great masses of people into the kingdom of God. In order for this prophecy to be fulfilled, the Iron Curtain had to fall, the Berlin Wall had to fall, and the Bamboo Curtain must be opened so more than one billion people of China can be free to respond to the good news of our Heavenly Father and our Lord Jesus Christ. You and I are eyewitnesses to the fulfillment of this prophecy.

I had the good fortune to be in West Germany, within an hour's drive of the crossover point between East and West Germany, when the Berlin Wall began to tumble. Talk about excitement! It was almost indescribable.

During our meetings in Munich, West Germany, we had East Berliners and others from East Germany coming over to worship with us. Their feet were scarcely touching the floor, they were so excited. For the prophecy of Isaiah and Micah to come to pass, the barriers of restriction had to come down. God is having His way.

2
I Will Pour Out
My Spirit
Upon All Flesh

What is the cause for the fall of the Berlin Wall and the Iron Curtain? We find the answer in Ezekiel 38:1-6.

> And the word of the Lord came unto me, saying, Son of man, set thy face against Gog, the land of Magog, the chief prince of Meshech and Tubal, and prophesy against him, and say, Thus saith the Lord God: Behold, I am against thee, O Gog, the chief prince of Meshech and Tubal:
>
> And I will turn thee back, and put hooks into thy jaws, and I will bring thee forth, and all thine army, horses and horsemen, all of them clothed with all sorts of armour, even a great company with bucklers and shields, all of them handling swords: Persia, Ethiopia, and Libya with them; all of them with shield and helmet: Gomer, and all his bands; the house of Togarmah of the north quarters, and all his bands: and many people with thee.

These verses identify the great northern power that is planning an eventual takeover of the tiny state of Israel. That great northern power is identified by the geographical areas of Magog, Meshech, and Tubal. The leader of the people of those lands is called Gog.

Notice in verses 2 and 3 that God, through the prophet, speaks to Gog, who is presently Mikhail Gorbachev. He says to him, I am against you. Whenever God directly declares

21

He is against someone, some land, or some evil operation, you must understand that they are in trouble!

It was a multitude of troubles that forced Mr. Gorbachev to become the architect of reform, openness, and change. It has come because he cannot help himself, and unless he and his followers turn to the Lord, they are going to be destroyed.

The making of reforms and the bringing about of change will not change Mikhail Gorbachev — only Jesus Christ can do that. But the reforms and changes benefit the masses of people. The Soviet Union, identified as Meshech, Magog, and Tubal, is in trouble.

They are in extremely serious trouble financially. For all practical purposes, they are bankrupt. They are in serious trouble agriculturally. They cannot feed their people without purchasing food from the western hemisphere.

They are in trouble because their people discovered the magnificent lifestyle of people within the western world. Communists, through the Iron Curtain, did their utmost to keep the influence and lifestyle of the western world away from the people in the Soviet Union. They failed.

The people have come to realize that the members of the Communist Party were an elite upper-class, while the remainder of the population are not much better off than the peasants during the days of Czar Nicholas and the czars before him. So, the Soviet Union — its government and leadership — is in serious trouble. Their military operations also have backfired in Afghanistan and Angola in West Africa.

The Deathblow for Communism

In the fall of 1956, I first preached from Ezekiel 38 and 39. My sermon title was, "God's Conquest of Russia." I later changed the title to "World War III." But in that first message, I declared that God had struck a deathblow to international communism. He had struck an irreparable blow and it would never be repaired.

The staggering blow came as the result of the 1956 atrocity in Hungary, in which the Soviets massacred over 50,000 people. The world was shocked by the brutality of the Soviets under Krushchev in 1956. The philosophy of that hour was peaceable coexistence. It was being heralded on our college and university campuses, by some politicians, by entertainers, and even by some members of the clergy.

Many sang the praises of communism in 1956. Soviet propaganda was taking a toll. But with the iron-fisted blows of the Soviets against the Hungarians, the world was shocked out of its stupor and made to realize that communism under Krushchev was just as brutal and ruthless as it had been under Stalin and Lenin.

God took advantage of that event to strike a deathblow to the foundation of international communism. It has never healed and today we are observing the dying gasps of this vicious political and philosophical beast.

Yes, Gorbachev and others will try to keep it alive, but a study of Ezekiel 38 and 39 reveals that this evil system does come to an absolute and total destruction.

Bible prophecies are an extremely interesting study, especially when they are being fulfilled. One of the first things I do in the morning, after thanking God for a good night's sleep, is to check the news, both by television and the newspaper, to discover what God has been doing while I slept.

We are living in a time when Bible prophecies are being fulfilled daily. There is not one major world event occurring today that is not the handiwork of Almighty God. His prophecies are coming to pass and with such accuracy it is like making sure you have dotted your "i's" and crossed your "t's" and used all the right punctuation.

The Fulfillment of Pentecost

Let's see if the prophets can tell us more about why we are witnessing this openness, change, and the destruction of the walls and barriers that have released almost one billion people. For most of these people, this is their first uninhibited opportunity to hear the Gospel and accept Jesus Christ.

The Prophet Joel provides additional insight in Joel 2:28-29. **And it shall come to pass afterward, that I will pour out my spirit upon all flesh; and your sons and your daughters shall prophesy, your old men shall dream dreams, your young men shall see visions.** See, he declares, And it shall come to pass. There's that term again. It causes me to know that the prophecy which follows is more certain than the rising and setting of the sun. The verse continues, **and it shall come to pass afterward.** I grew up in the church and never heard a prophetic teacher touch the word "afterward." It was passed over. But the text clearly says, **It shall come to pass afterward.** In other words, after other things have been fulfilled, then Joel's prophecy will be completely fulfilled.

Keep the word "afterward" in mind; we will return to it. Joel continues, **I will pour out my spirit upon all flesh.** Please notice the extent of the prophecy, on all flesh. We have not had such a dimension of outpouring to date. Tie Joel's prophecy to Isaiah 2:2 and Micah 4:1 — that people from all nations will flow into the kingdom of God in the last days. This is exciting! The Prophet Joel prophesies an outpouring of the Holy Spirit on all flesh which is yet to be fulfilled.

Let's examine the fulfillment of Joel's prophecy to date. Everyone in the Upper Room on the Jewish feast day of Pentecost, more than 1,900 years ago, was Jewish. The crowd which the spiritual event attracted was Jewish. Peter's great sermon was preached to a Jewish crowd. The early Church was all Jewish for the first decade.

Gentiles did not begin to make their way into the Church until God sent Peter down to Cornelius' house, as recorded in Acts 10. Then they began to be part of the Church and today they are the major part of the Church.

Think about this important fact — the only places on earth where men and women can learn about and experience the outpouring of the Holy Spirit is where a preacher, a teacher, or a missionary has been sent by God with this message. There are people living in your own immediate neighborhood who do not know about the Holy Spirit. While many people in the United States have heard about the Holy Spirit, millions still have not heard and are ignorant of the subject.

But go abroad and you'll find that the masses of people do not know that there is a Holy Spirit. The Prophet Joel said the Holy Spirit shall be poured out on all flesh. Isaiah and Micah agree. Joel's prophecy says our sons and daughters will prophesy, and our old men will dream dreams. These are divinely given dreams, designed to become reality.

Young men will see visions — divinely given visions, designed to become reality. And he said on men servants and women servants, people of high estate and low estate, He will pour out His Spirit in those days. We know this prophecy began to be fulfilled on the Jewish feast day of Pentecost, but the prophecy was not totally fulfilled there.

That was only the beginning. This prophecy of Joel's cannot be totally fulfilled until the Holy Spirit is poured out on all flesh and is causing people of all nations to flow into the kingdom of God. We're not talking about a trickling in, not just a few hundred or a few thousand, but a flowing of multitudes of people into the kingdom of God.

The description calls us to envision a mighty river out of its banks. This powerful flow of water is such that man has nothing available to stop it. He can only wait until the flow subsides.

God has chosen words carefully to give us a picture of what is going to happen — a mighty river out of its banks, flowing and carrying everything in its path right along with it. That's what God is revealing to us through this prophecy.

It has been prophesied and has begun to come to pass. But in order for it to come to pass, the Iron Curtain and the Berlin Wall had to come down. And the Bamboo Curtain in the Orient will come down. Praise God, this is exciting! God is having His way! The greatest day of the outpouring of the Holy Spirit is in our immediate future. It is imminent.

3

The Soviet Future

Before we elaborate on the prophetic future of the Soviet Union, let's look at the geographic areas mentioned in the Scriptures. The opening verses of Ezekiel 38:1-3 speak of Gog, Magog, Meshech, and Tubal — all of which are identified with the Soviet Union.

And the word of the Lord came unto me, saying, Son of man, set thy face against Gog, the land of Magog, the chief prince of Meshech and Tubal, and prophesy against him, and say, Thus saith the Lord God: Behold, I am against thee, O Gog, the chief prince of Meshech and Tubal.

In Genesis 10:1,2, we learn that Magog, Meshech, and Tubal were grandsons of Noah. **Now these are the generations of the sons of Noah, Shem, Ham, and Japheth: and unto them were sons born after the flood. The sons of Japheth; Gomer, and Magog, and Madai, and Javan, and Tubal, and Meshech, and Tiras.** They, with their expanding families, migrated northward, above the nation of Israel, and settled in the ancient lands of Scythia. Ancient Scythia and the provinces of Magog, Meshech, and Tubal are today within the boundaries of the Soviet Union.

The term "Gog" mentioned in Ezekiel 38:2 identifies the political leader of that land, presently Mikhail Gorbachev. Verse 5 speaks of Persia, Ethiopia, and Libya. These areas are influentially dominated by the Soviet Union and will still be linked with the Soviets at the time of their attempted military takeover of the tiny nation of Israel.

Persia of Ezekiel's day is presently known as Iran. But in those days the area of Persia was much larger than present-day Iran, also including the area we know today as Iraq. The nation of Iraq is identified with the Babylonian Empire.

The Babylonian Empire preceded the Persian Empire described in Daniel, chapter 2. Ezekiel, along with all Israel, was taken into captivity by the Babylonian Empire. However, the Persian Empire swallowed up the Babylonians and the captivity of Israel continued on.

So the Persian Empire was made up of geographical areas that, today, can be identified as Iraq and Iran. Both of these nations have been prominent in the news in recent years. The world witnessed their devastating eight-year war with each other in the '80s. Iraq won that war and more recently invaded Kuwait in its efforts to dominate the Arab world.

The Soviets are not yet in absolute control of Iraq and Iran, but they are a major influence in Iraq due to the military treaties of 1972. According to Bible prophecy (Ezek. 38:5), the Soviet takeover of Iran (or Persia as it was then known) is inevitable.

Notice that some of the upheaval in the Soviet Union is in republics bordering Iran. The prophetic verses in Ezekiel 38 enable us to better understand what's happening in our world. It is revealed in the Book of Ezekiel, written more than 2,600 years ago, how this prophet of God spoke about world affairs of our present day. The Soviet Union did not exist 2,600 years ago — the communists only took over that area in 1917, 1918 — yet it is identified in these prophetic scriptures.

The nation of Ethiopia is under communist control due to the Marxist takeover in November 1977. And Libya, on the coast of North Africa, is a communist puppet state today.

28

The major influence in Libya has been the Soviet Union through the military treaties of 1952.

The world is well aware that Kaddafi is one of the puppets of Moscow, along with Arafat of the PLO, and Castro of Cuba. They have been militarily provided for by the Soviet Union.

The Role of Germany

Ezekiel 38:6 speaks of Gomer, and all his bands. **Gomer, and all his bands; the house of Togarmah of the north quarters, and all his bands: and many people with thee.** The ancient province of Gomer is presently identified with the geographic region we now call Eastern Europe — the countries of East Germany, Poland, Hungary, and Czechoslovakia.

The Soviet Union gained domination of this area in 1949, after World War II, when Europe was divided by the "big three" — Churchill, Truman, and Stalin.

Following the collapse of Soviet communism and the fall of the Berlin Wall, it was inevitable that the two Germanies would reunite, as they did in 1990. That, however, will not affect the prophecy of God's Word. There will still be a major part of ancient Gomer under Soviet domination when the Soviets move against Israel.

Do not expect the Soviet Union to completely release the nations to which it is now giving reform. In spite of this reform, which allows some freedom to the people of Eastern European nations, the Soviets will continue to be the dominant military force. Even so, God is having His way for the sake of His people.

Mr. Gorbachev is not going to relinquish control, giving the people absolute and total release. Should he do so, his days would be numbered. His successor would move swiftly into position to continue military dominance.

How long will the doors to the harvest fields of the Soviet Union and the Eastern European nations remain wide open? We do not know. We do know they will be open long enough for the Church to invade with the Gospel of Jesus Christ and sweep multiplied millions into the Kingdom of God!

This means that we, as Christians, have our work cut out for us — the opportunity of soul-winning on a major scale. But the Body of Christ is capable and we have the resources. We have the troops and we can do it!

The Role of Turkey

Ezekiel 38:6 speaks of the house of **Togarmah, of the north quarters, and all his bands: and many people with thee.** Who is modern-day Togarmah? The ancient lands of Togarmah include the nations of Romania, Bulgaria, and Turkey. Romania and Bulgaria came under Soviet control in 1949. According to biblical prophecy, Turkey will also come under Soviet domination.

Watch carefully — it's in the Book and it will come to pass. Notice the fourth verse of Ezekiel 38. The emphasis is on the military. God speaks through the prophet, concerning the Soviet Union, **I will turn thee around, and put hooks into thy jaws, and I will bring thee forth, and all thine army, horses and horsemen, all of them clothed with all sorts of armour, even a great company with bucklers and shields, all of them handling swords.**

All the nations listed in verses 5 and 6 have military equipment and troops, and again great emphasis is placed on the military. Verse 7 addresses Magog, Meshech, and Tubal and their leader (presently Gorbachev) — **Be thou prepared.** This statement speaks of military preparation.

To believe that the reforms and the present openness of the Soviet Union means they will militarily disarm is very naive.

So Ezekiel warns — Be on guard: **Be thou prepared, and prepare for thyself, thou, and all thy company that are assembled unto thee, and be thou a guard unto them.**

No one should be deceived into thinking the Soviet Union is going to disarm because of the new reforms. Certainly they have made no attempts to do so to date.

God's Prophecies for Russia

Verse 8 continues, **After many days thou shalt be visited.** God is saying, "I will have My way. I am not going to stop having My way. I am going to visit you." God is prophesying, through the Prophet Ezekiel, concerning the Soviet Union.

After many days you will be called to arms. In future years you will invade a land that has recovered from war, whose people were gathered from many nations to the mountains of Israel, which had long been desolate. They had been brought out from the nations, and now all of them live in safety.

Ezekiel 38:8 NIV

This is a direct description of this powerful military machine taking action against the new nation of Israel.

You will remember from your biblical studies that when Moses and the children of Israel arrived at the border of Canaan, Moses sent 12 spies on into the land. He told them to stay in the land 40 days and then return and report.

They did so. And when they returned, they declared, "The land flows with milk and honey and we brought samples of the fruit and produce" (It was like none they had ever seen before.) (See Num. 13:27.)

The children of Israel did not occupy the land at that time because of their fear and unbelief. However, the land remained rich, fertile, and highly productive when they occupied it 40 years later. During the time they occupied the land and were obedient to God, the land continued to

31

flow with milk and honey, and the produce was the finest on the earth.

The Destruction of the Promised Land

But with the captivity of the children of Israel because of their disobedience to God, deterioration of the land began to take place. During the thousands of years the lands were occupied by Babylonians, Persians, Greeks, Romans, Ottomans, and Turks, they were stripped of all of their magnificent forests, the topsoil eroded away, and the fertile lands were reduced to nothing more than malaria-filled swamps and sand dunes.

During World War I, the British took over the Middle East. In 1919, they sent their top agriculturalists to the land to analyze the soil throughout all of the area that was once ancient Israel.

They returned to England, declaring, ''The land is unfit for human habitation.'' Then, World War II came with the holocaust and the Jews began their move back to the land of their fathers. The British, who controlled the area, resisted the Jews' return because they feared they would starve to death.

The Jewish people returning to Israel after World War II were not known for their agricultural ability, and they were returning to lands that were unfit to live on. The country was desolate and barren, producing almost nothing. Ezekiel, chapter 36, presents some amazing information. It is one of the most revealing chapters in all of God's Word, describing the restoration of the land of ancient Israel. Ezekiel 36:10-12:

> And I will multiply men upon you, all the house of Israel, even all of it: and the cities shall be inhabited, and the wastes shall be builded: and I will multiply upon you man and beast; and they shall increase and bring fruit: and I will settle you after your old estates,

and will do better unto you than at your beginnings: and ye shall know that I am the Lord.

Yea, I will cause men to walk upon you, even my people Israel; and they shall possess thee, and thou shalt be their inheritance, and thou shalt no more henceforth bereave them of men.

God reveals how the land will be restored and exactly who will bring about the restoration. Ezekiel says the land will be "tilled and sown by the house of Israel, even all of them." (See Ezek. 36:10-12 above).

And that is exactly what has happened! I could take you to Israel today and show you beautiful forests. Northwest of Bersheeba, in the Lahav Desert area, our ministry helped plant trees in the desert sand in 1978. Today, I can stand in the shade of those trees. It is exciting to climb the five-story fire tower and view the surrounding area. Many areas have been reforested and it is an absolute fulfillment of prophecy.

Trees hold topsoil and increase rainfall. Israel's land today is rich, fertile, and highly productive.

Peace and Safety for Israel?

Has Israel, at any time in her more than 42 years of existence, ever dwelt safely? No. Is she presently dwelling safely? No. But the scripture says she will be dwelling safely prior to the attempted Soviet takeover.

The news programs quite often print reports on the conditions in Israel. One such report involved two of my friends in the Israeli government — Prime Minister Yitzak Shamir and Vice-Prime Minister and Foreign Minister Shimon Peres.

I met Mr. Peres many years ago, before he became Prime Minister. He was the leader of the labor party and continued to serve during the time of Menachem Begin.

What the world does not know is that David Ben-Gurion, the "father of modern Israel," hand-picked Shimon Peres to become the most outstanding leader of the new nation of Israel. In his own handwriting, Ben-Gurion says, "Shimon, be patient. Study, learn well. Shimon, always keep in mind, we are not here by our will; we are here by the will of the Almighty." Powerful letters — I saw them myself. Shimon pulled them from the files in his office in Tel Aviv.

The handiwork of God in Israel is absolutely colossal. But today there is much controversy among the political leaders. The whole government is being threatened because the people want to see some concrete steps toward bringing about a more peaceful condition between themselves and the Arabs. And the Scripture prophesies, **They will be dwelling safely.**

For Israel to dwell safely, they not only must resolve their internal problems, but they also must have peace with Lebanon. Lebanon has been ripped apart by nearly two decades of civil strife. Presently Syria has gained the upper hand in Lebanon. Peace must come to Lebanon and a stable government must arise in order for them to make peace with Israel. Syria, Jordan and Saudi Arabia must also make peace with Israel. Egypt is already at peace with Israel. A majority of the Arab nations must make peace with Israel in order for Israel to dwell safely.

Ezekiel 38:11 describes what will happen — **Thou shalt say** (speaking to the Soviets) — **I will go to them that are at rest, that dwell safely, all of them dwelling without walls, and having neither bars nor gates.**

This verse reveals the degree of peace that will develop. Peace will be so welcome, by both sides, that Israel will not only be dwelling safely, but will have no need to defend or protect herself against her neighbors.

It is prophesied. God said it and it will come to pass!

The Soviet Attack

Once this period of peace and safety has settled in, the Soviets will make their move. **Thou shalt ascend and come like a storm, thou shalt be like a cloud to cover the land** (Ezek. 38:9). Notice that God gave accurate insight to the prophets of the Old Testament.

One of the most powerful forces of the Soviet military is their rapid deployment force. They move more troops and equipment faster than any other nation on the earth.

In November of 1977, the Soviet Union moved three combined armies and all their equipment from their Black Sea bases, via Libya, into Ethiopia in ten hours, where they completed the takeover of that nation. To do that, they had to violate the air space of five sovereign nations. All those nations protested the next morning at the U.N. in New York City. But as so often is the case, the U.N. did nothing.

This event occurred when the eyes of the world were focused on Jerusalem. Anwar Sadat, of Egypt, had gone to Israel and Jerusalem to visit Menachem Begin, where he addressed the Knesset. And the Soviets chose that specific time to make their move on Ethiopia.

This historical event was not reported by the American press until nine years later.

The USSR later explained that their move was a simple military exercise. Having achieved their goal, they quickly withdrew.

Ezekiel 38:4 speaks of the army coming forth on horses. In Ezekiel's day, the best means for transporting the military was by horseback. Soldiers wore various types of armor and used ancient weapons. Armies do not travel by horse today, nor do they use these ancient weapons. So the Soviets will not come against Israel riding on four-footed beasts. The initial thrust against Israel is going to be by air.

No damage is done to the Word of God by the updating of military transportation and weapons. The important thing is to have consistent interpretation of Scripture. Just as we recognize modern-day geographical names, we must also recognize that fast-moving mechanized armored vehicles have replaced horses.

Thus saith the Lord God; It shall also come to pass, that at the same time shall things come into thy mind, and thou shalt think an evil thought (Ezek. 38:10). In other words, you (the Soviet Union) will make an evil plan.

The Soviet Union's Evil Plan

There can be no question, the Soviet Union has an evil plan. Communism has wrecked the Soviet Union and proved to be a destructive ideology. For all practical reasons communism has failed and is dead. But don't be fooled by perestroika and glasnost. God is presently having His way for the benefit of the oppressed people. But there is an ulterior motive hidden in the Soviet plans. The Word of God says, "It's an evil plan." This is not a report from ABC, CBS, or NBC — nor is it from your local newspapers. It is from God's Word — and that's the bottom line.

The Soviets will be confronted by those who support Israel. They will ask, Why are you coming? Why are you doing this? What is your interest in the nation of Israel? Verse 12 gives us the answer, **To take a spoil, and to take a prey; to turn thine hand upon the desolate places that are now inhabited, and upon the people that are gathered out of the nations, which have gotten cattle and goods, that dwell in the midst of the land.**

What is the Soviet's desire? They want the livestock and goods of this land. Israel produces more food per acre than any other nation on this planet, including ours. In Eliat, the southern-most city of Israel, a prophesied agricultural miracle is taking place.

36

The city of Eliat is the hub of the Araba Desert . . . the exact desert of which Isaiah prophesied . . . **the desert shall rejoice, and blossom as the rose. It shall blossom abundantly** (Isa. 35:1,2). In the original language, it says, "And the Araba Desert shall blossom like the rose. It shall blossom abundantly."

One may observe phenomenal agricultural development there in the desert sands at any time of the year. During the special season, tomato plants produce as much as 80 tons of tomatoes per acre. Nowhere else on earth is that possible. Eggplants, bell peppers, and onions grow equally as well. The date trees also produce more per acre than anywhere else on earth.

The finest dairy herds in all the earth are now in Israel. Dairy cattle there are prima donnas. They have the finest care and feeding. The cattle produce more milk, with higher fat content, than anywhere on earth.

In the past decade, Israel has developed an impressive cattle industry — producing some of the finest beef ever eaten. The industry not only supplies the people of Israel, but they are now exporting beef, also.

On the other hand, the Soviet Union is plagued with trouble. It comes in various forms and from every direction. One of the major problems confronting the Soviet government is the lack of food! They cannot feed their people. Their agriculture is in a shambles. Nature does not seem to cooperate with them. In the past 21 growing seasons, they have had 17 crop failures — some extreme, some very minor. But they are unable to produce a sufficient amount of food to feed their growing population.

The communists, under Marx and Lenin, used hungry people to overthrow the czar in 1917,1918. They marshaled the hungry masses, and overthrew the czar — then began their expansion. The same thing that threatened and brought down the czar, now threatens communism —

hunger. And it will get worse before it gets better. The Soviets need food and soon they will be desperate. Eventually, the lack of food will become extremely critical. Then the Soviets will risk a major war in order to take over Israel because of its ability to produce vast supplies of food.

The Russian-Israeli Conflict

Ezekiel 38:13 reveals the opposition to the Soviet's evil plan.

> **Sheba, and Dedan** (the Arab nations that will have made peace with Israel and will be enjoying that relationship), **and the merchants of Tarshish, with all the young lions thereof, shall say unto thee, Art thou come to take a spoil? Hast thou gathered thy company to take a prey? To carry away silver and gold, to take away cattle and goods, to take a great spoil?**

The merchants of Tarshish are presently identified as the Common Market. Tarshish was the second largest Mediterranean port in Ezekiel's day. Merchants from the area we know as Europe and the Middle East traded at Tarshish and became known as the merchants of Tarshish. The modern-day counterpart is the Common Market.

The young lions — Australia, Canada, New Zealand, South Africa, and the United States — are the offspring of the great British Empire.

When Rome collapsed, the system of ancient empires came to an end. The next major empire to arise was Great Britain. Their symbol was, and still is, the lion. How did the British Empire differ from all which preceded it? The empires from Egypt to Rome were all controlled by Satan. With the rise of the British Empire, missionaries began to spread the Gospel around the world. That's quite a difference!

Since the young lions are identified with Great Britain, the USA must certainly be included.

Which lion leads the pack? Not the oldest lion, but the strongest young lion, the United States of America.

Which nation of the young lions is the major supporter of Israel? The United States of America!

Remember, God said to Abraham, in Genesis 12:3, **I will bless them that bless thee, and curse him that curseth thee.** Although Americans may not always agree with how the nation of Israel conducts their internal business, we must maintain our support, for it is this support that assures us of God's blessings. The young lions will still be supporting Israel when the Soviets attempt a military takeover of the state of Israel.

This will bring about a military confrontation. Will it be nuclear? Yes. Some will say, "That could be tragic!" Well, it could be, but it won't.

Ezekiel 38:15:

> **And thou shalt come from thy place out of the north parts, thou, and many people with thee, all of them riding upon horses, a great company, and a mighty army** (The Soviet Union is about as far north of Israel as it can be). **And thou shalt come up against my people of Israel, as a cloud to cover the land; it shall be in the latter days, and I will bring thee against my land, that the heathen may know me, when I shall be sanctified in thee, O Gog,** (Gorbachev, or whoever may succeed him), **before their eyes.**

> **Art thou he of whom I have spoken in old time by my servants the prophets of Israel, which prophesied in those days many years that I would bring thee against them? And it shall come to pass at the same time when Gog** (the Soviet leader) **shall come against the land of Israel, saith the Lord God, that my fury will come up in my face. For in my jealousy and in the fire of my wrath have I spoken.**

God will protect Israel from the Soviet Union and their combined forces. He will defend them with His wrath!

No one living in the era of the Church has ever witnessed the wrath of God. The Prophet Nahum, speaking to the people of Israel in their captivity, declared that God reserves His wrath for His enemies. This means the Jews will be spared (see Nah. 1:2).

When Jesus introduced God's grace, God's wrath was put on hold, where it will remain until this prophesied event. This will be the first event to evoke God's wrath since He laid it aside. And when God turns to wrath, you don't want to be in His path.

However, God will not turn His wrath against the Soviet Union until the Jewish population has departed the Soviet Union. God's covenant with Abraham, Isaac, and Jacob, to give Canaan to Israel is for one thousand generations (see Ps. 105:7-11). So we know that God has continued plans for Israel. We are now observing the unfolding of some of those plans while others will unfold during the millenium.

Matthew 1:17 declares that from the time of Abraham to Jesus, only 42 of the 1,000 generations have passed. To date, almost 100 generations have passed. So God's covenant with Israel still has more than 900 generations to last. God's covenant with Israel stands to this very day. Run biblical references on the word "covenant" and determine the certainty of God's Word.

God's Covenant Continues

Pay no attention to ANY teacher who declares the covenant with Israel is broken. If that is so, then God's Word has been violated. And if Satan succeeded in violating the Word of God in this instance, then no one would know when it might be violated again. What would that do to your faith? It would utterly destroy it!

Some teachers say, "The old covenant has been broken. It has been done away with. We have a better covenant now." We do have a better covenant — but our better covenant does not cancel another truth in God's Word.

The Devil tries to cause disbelief by saying that parts of God's Word are no longer valid. And if he can get you to believe that one part of the Scripture is no longer effective, you can be sure he'll try to convince you that other parts of God's Word are not valid.

But the covenant remains and the wrath of God is reserved for His enemies. Before God can pour out His wrath upon the Soviet Union and their allies, to prevent them from taking over Israel, there must be an exodus of the Jewish people from the Soviet Union.

Are the Jewish people leaving the Soviet Union? They are moving out by the tens of thousands! Arguments involving Israel and the PLO as to where Soviet Jews may settle in Israel have made front-page news.

The Soviet Union would like to see them settling in America. But Israel says, "No. They belong to us." And Israel is the safest place for the Soviet Jews.

Have you ever wondered why Gorbachev's predecessors died as rapidly as they did? I believe it was because they resisted a release of the Jewish people. Wisely, Gorbachev has seen the handwriting on the wall.

I am confident that the same angel who delivered the children of Israel out of Pharaoh's grasp in Egypt — the Death Angel — hovers over the Kremlin. Gorbachev will either be the man to release the Jews, or there will be another state funeral in the Soviet Union.

Get Ready for the Rapture

Thank God, the Jewish exodus has begun. Israel is now hard-pressed to provide living quarters for the more than one million people coming from the Soviet Union. This is not sensationalism or fantasy — the exodus has begun.

41

First Thessalonians 5:9 speaks to the Church, **For God hath not appointed us to wrath, but to obtain salvation by our Lord Jesus Christ.** Before God can pour out His wrath upon the Soviet Union and bring massive devastation to that region, He must remove the Church from that area.

There is only one vehicle designed by God for the removal of the Church — it is called rapture, or — **to be received by Jesus** (John 14:3), — **caught up to meet the Lord in the air** (1 Thess. 4:16-18), — **or gathered together unto the Lord** (2 Thess. 2:1).

God must first snatch the Church away. So once the Jewish people have departed the Soviet Union and the Church is caught away, God will destroy the Soviet Union.

For in my jealousy and in the fire of my wrath have I spoken, Surely in that day there shall be a great shaking (a great earthquake — one that will probably measure 8 or above on the Richter scale, given the damage described) **in the land of Israel** (Ezek. 38:19). This Scripture speaks of the land of Israel, not the state of Israel that we know, for God is defending Israel. The exact boundaries of Israel are found in Genesis 15:18, **In the same day the Lord made a covenant with Abram, saying, Unto thy seed have I given this land, from the river of Egypt unto the great river, the river Euphrates** (the northern border of the land of Israel). (See the map.)

The river of Egypt is the Nile River. That means that southern Iraq, Syria, Jordan, Saudi Arabia, the Sinai Peninsula, and the land east of the River Nile, belong to Israel by the decree of Almighty God. So this Scripture is identifying a vast area of land — not the state of Israel as we presently know it.

A major earthquake could occur in the land of Israel and still be far enough north so as not to harm the nation of Israel. After all, God is defending present day Israel — not destroying it. But the entire earth will have tremors

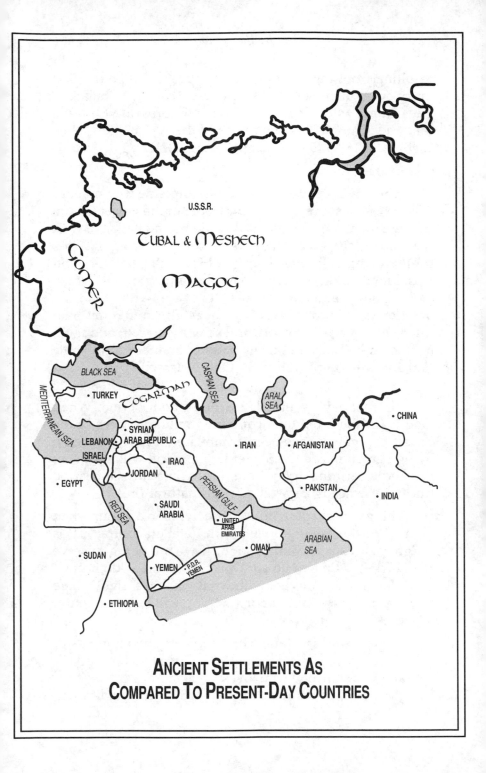

**ANCIENT SETTLEMENTS AS
COMPARED TO PRESENT-DAY COUNTRIES**

resulting from this mighty earthquake. It will be the first major event in the seven-year period we call the Tribulation. The Church will be in heaven. The Scriptures do NOT teach that the Church will go through the Tribulation. (See 1 Thess. 4:16-18; 5:9-11 and 2 Thess. 2:1-12.)

Ezekiel continues:

And I will call for a sword (an implement of military warfare) **against him** (Gog — the leader of the Soviet Union) **throughout all my mountains** (kingdoms and nations), **saith the Lord God: every man's sword shall be against his brother. And I will plead against him with pestilence and with blood; and I will rain upon him, and upon his bands, and upon the many people that are with him, an overflowing rain, and great hailstones, fire, and brimstone. Thus will I magnify myself, and sanctify myself; and I will be known in the eyes of many nations, and they shall know that I am the Lord** (the Holy One in Israel).

Ezekiel 38:21-23

"In that day" — one day. One 24-hour period. When God is finished, the total combined military forces of the Soviet Union will have been annihilated. There will be no living person inside the Soviet Union. God will have sent fire and brimstone upon them — possibly missile-bearing nuclear warheads, as well as supernatural fire.

Things are shaping up. We are living in an hour when God's Word is being fulfilled with detailed accuracy. It is a sign that Jesus is coming soon. If we are going to serve the Lord, it is time to do so. Don't put it off — do it now! Start doing what you can, with what you have, right where you are right now, not tomorrow! You will be in the center of God's will.

I once heard Dr. James Brown, a Presbyterian pastor from Pennsylvania, give the definition of a fanatic. He said, "A fanatic is someone who loves Jesus more than you do." So, go right ahead and serve the Lord with commitment, discipline, and diligence. More than likely, someone will think you are a fanatic. Accept that identity with joy!

Remember, Jesus said to the lukewarm Church in Revelation, chapter 3. "I'd rather that you were cold or hot." Do not be lukewarm or a compromiser. It is time to pull out the stops. If you don't have your spiritual armor on, according to Ephesians 6:13, get it on. **Wherefore take unto you the whole armour of God, that ye may be able to withstand in the evil day, and having done all, to stand.** If you're not using weapons of God's warfare to pull down strongholds (2 Cor. 10:4), check out your weapons. **For the weapons of our warfare are not carnal, but mighty through God to the pulling down of strong holds.** If you haven't recognized the fact that you have been enlisted by the Lord Jesus Christ and that you are a part of God's army on this earth, then get into the writings of Paul to Timothy and discover your position. Then, report for duty.

4
The Coming World Harvest

In 1981, the Holy Spirit directed me to study the Word of God and put together a message which I entitled, "The Dam Breaks." That message was based on Isaiah 2:2, **And it shall come to pass in the last days, that the mountain of the Lord's house shall be established in the top of the mountains, and shall be exalted above the hills; and all nations shall flow unto it,** and Micah 4:1, **But in the last days it shall come to pass, that the mountain of the house of the Lord shall be established in the top of the mountains, and it shall be exalted above the hills; and people shall flow unto it.** Through those passages, God declared there would come a breaking of a great barrier which had been withholding masses of people from His kingdom and that once the barrier was removed, people would flow into the kingdom of God.

Then, when the nation of Israel became forty years old, on May 15, 1988, the Holy Spirit directed me to put together another message from Joel 2:22-29.

> Be not afraid, ye beasts of the field: for the pastures of the wilderness do spring, for the tree beareth her fruit, the fig tree and the vine do yield their strength. Be glad then, ye children of Zion, and rejoice in the Lord your God: for He hath given you the former rain moderately, and He will cause to come down for you the rain, the former rain, and the latter rain in the first month. And the floors shall be full of wheat, and the vats shall overflow with wine and oil.

47

And I will restore to you the years that the locust hath eaten, the cankerworm, and the caterpiller, and the palmerworm, my great army which I sent among you. And ye shall eat in plenty, and be satisfied, and praise the name of the Lord your God, that hath dealt wondrously with you: and My people shall never be ashamed. And ye shall know that I am in the midst of Israel, and that I am the Lord your God, and none else: and My people shall never be ashamed.

And it shall come to pass afterward, that I will pour out My spirit upon all flesh; and your sons and your daughters shall prophesy, your old men shall dream dreams, your young men shall see visions: and also upon the servants and upon the handmaids in those days will I pour out My spirit.

I entitled that message, "Afterward Comes the Outpouring."

A Gathering of Wild Animals

These prophecies state that after God begins the restoration of the nation of Israel, it will progress to such a degree that wild animals will voluntarily return to the nation of Israel (see Joel 2:22). And with this occurrence, a massive outpouring of the Holy Spirit upon all flesh, worldwide, will soon follow.

Within the last decade, wild animals began returning to the nation of Israel voluntarily. In recent years, both the lion and the bear have been seen in the forests of Israel. Many other species of wild animals such as deer, gazelle, and the ibex, now roam the countryside.

There is only one other reference in God's Word where wild animals were directed by God. Genesis 7 tells how animals voluntarily boarded Noah's Ark. Think about it, when wild animals begin to be obedient to the will of God, it is time for every child of God to walk in strict obedience to Him.

Signs of the End Time Abound

I am called by the Holy Spirit and gifted to work with the prophecy of the Scripture. The Holy Spirit gives me excellent understanding and insight into coming prophetic events. Early in 1989, I preached from Luke 21:25, where Jesus prophesied of the coming distress of nations, with perplexity, because of the roaring and tossing of the sea and the waves. The verse reads, **And there shall be signs in the sun, and in the moon, and in the stars; and upon the earth distress of nations, with perplexity; the sea and the waves roaring.**

Signs in the sun and moon refer to the space program, not astronomy. The scientific record of the astronomer will show that the sun, moon, and stars do nothing but what they are programmed to do by God. They do a number of different things, but they do them in cycles, repeating themselves over various time frames. Signs in the sun, moon, and stars are the effects of our space program — man thrusting himself into God's front yard.

When Jesus prophesied, He always prophesied in perfect chronological order. You notice in Luke 21:24, He prophesied there would be a time when the city of Jerusalem would no longer be controlled by Gentiles. That occurred on June 7, 1967, during the Six Day War, when the armies of Israel repossessed the ancient city of Jerusalem.

In 1968, our space program took astronauts into orbit around the moon, 240,000 miles from the earth's surface. In 1969, two astronauts walked on the moon, and in 1971, astronauts drove on the moon.

Manmade signs in the sun, moon, and stars followed the end of the Gentile reign over Jerusalem. Since that time, we have been examining all the major planets in our galaxy, putting up all kinds of vehicles, some that stay in close orbit, others that orbit as far as 25,000 miles out in space

49

The understanding of signs in the sun, moon, and stars has to do with the activities of our space program and those of other nations. But notice, at the same time on the earth, there is distress of nations, with perplexity. The words "distress" and "perplexity" as used in this text indicate nations that are greatly embarrassed over internal problems caused by the sea and the waves roaring.

Allow the Word of God to interpret itself. Here the words "sea" and "waves" are used symbolically. When the word "sea" is used in the Bible and a body of water is not identified, the word "sea" indicates masses of people.

This Scripture says there will be distress of nations, with perplexity; the sea and the waves roaring. You and I know there have not been monstrous activities on large bodies of water which threaten the destruction of nations, nor shall there ever be because of God's covenant in Genesis 9:13.

We also know that masses of people began serious demonstrations about the same time Jerusalem was being repossessed by Israel. The space program was developing and masses of people were demonstrating. Today, demonstrations on every continent have brought distress of one sort or another to virtually every nation on the earth. We are living in a great day of prophecy.

We are witnessing masses of humanity, like a sea of people, in great demonstrations, such as those here in the United States in the 1960s and 1970s. Such demonstrations continue today, creating problems for our government that are extremely difficult to solve.

Massive demonstrations are occurring in South Korea, the Philippines, Africa, Israel, Lebanon, Europe, China, and now, in Eastern Europe and the Soviet Union. Nations long under the control of the Soviet Union are anxious for absolute liberty, which is bringing about distress and perplexity.

What Will Happen Next?

Without question, our day is described in the prophecies of Jesus. Bible prophecy as it relates to world affairs is a most important subject for the Church at this present time. Let's look at some absolute facts and figures that are important.

The people of the Soviet Union were oppressed for seventy-one years. The Communist Revolution, which began under Karl Marx and Vladimir Lenin, finished its first phase in 1918. The Russian people and the other republics that the Soviets would soon swallow up, remained under communist domination for seventy-one years, from 1918 to 1989.

Imagine seventy-one years of oppression. There was the constant threat of imprisonment, and children were taught there is no God except the state. Religious freedom was suppressed. Christians often had no more than a verse of Scripture torn from a Bible to share with others. With the reforms of perestroika, the church bells of the Soviet Union were permitted to ring on Easter morning and Christmas morning in 1989 for the first time in seventy-one years.

The people of East Germany, Poland, Hungary, Romania, Czechoslovakia, and Bulgaria also suffered the same type of oppression, restraint, and threats for forty years.

Now, after forty years, they, too, are enjoying reforms, changes, and freedoms. During the most intense years of the Communist Revolution in Russia and her neighboring republics, it has been reported that more than seventy-five million Chinese were executed either for their resistance or because they were Christians.

What a tremendous price has been paid by the people of these regions. But today there is release and reform — a fresh breath of air is beginning to come to them. Dr. Deng

Ziaoping of China has ordered all of the churches to be reopened. Reforms are slowly coming about in China.

The upheaval of more than a million Chinese students in the months of May, and June, 1989, and the tragedy of Tiananmen Square were a setback for the movement of reform and change in China. However, President Bush, with amazing wisdom, sent several top statesmen to China to get democracy back on track. Our president has been severely criticized for his actions, and yet, God is having His way. These great world leaders are unaware that their actions are playing into the hands of God and bringing about the fulfillment of His Word. When God is ready for His Word to be fulfilled, He does not have to ask their permission.

God controls the directions taken by world leaders that open the doors for the blessings He wants the people to enjoy.

The Field is the World

Consider the statement of Jesus, **Do you not say, there are still four months and then comes the harvest? Behold I say to you, lift up your eyes and look at the fields, for they are already white for harvest!** (John 4:35 NKJV).

With today's tremendous change, reforms, and openness, I tell you, there are worldwide harvest fields ready to be harvested. It is an extremely important assignment to take advantage of the moment and reach out to the masses of people with the message of Jesus.

Consider the population of the Warsaw Pact nations — Poland, 39 million; Hungary, 10.8 million; Bulgaria, 9.4 million; Romania, 23.9 million; East Germany, 16.6 million; Czechoslovakia, 16 million. These people are now free to receive the Word, along with the 330 million from the Soviet Union.

52

There are other nations influenced by communism that are now affected by perestroika and glasnost. Yugoslavia, with 23.9 million, is forced to make changes which leave them open for the Gospel. Albania, with 3.4 million, and Soviet-controlled Ethiopia with 42.7 million, provide other new opportunities to preach the Gospel.

The list goes on — Angola in West Africa, 10 million; Libya, 4.3 million; Cuba, 10.5 million. All these peoples will be affected by what Mr. Gorbachev is doing, because God is having His way. At this writing, some of the leaders of these nations are not yet in agreement with Mr. Gorbachev and are making no overtures to accept change. However, he has stated if they want his continued support, they must come along. So we will wait and see how these leaders respond.

Consider this: China's population in 1989 was 1,119,600,000. North Korea, 22,400,000; Vietnam, 65,400,000. Think about it! Look at all these millions in the Orient who will be affected by the change that is coming about. China will lead the way, because God is having His way.

We must pray that the change which has begun in China will not be hindered but will fully develop and affect all other Oriental nations. That adds up to about 1.7 billion — in the Orient alone. And there are other areas which are still restricted, such as middle and southern Asia. This is the Moslem and Hindu population, which amounts to 1.3 billion.

Considering the oriental world, along with the Moslems, Hindus, those in the Soviet Union, the eastern European nations, and other communist countries, such as Ethiopia, Albania, Angola, Cuba, etc., this is a grand total of almost 3 billion people. This figure is approximately two-thirds of the earth's population. Of this amount, more than half are now open to the Gospel. And, you can be sure,

God will open the door to the remainder. Remember, God is having His way. The Gospel must be preached to the ends of the earth.

Watch for the open doors. Since God has brought down the Iron Curtain, the Berlin Wall, and is opening the Bamboo Curtain, we know that He is already at work, penetrating the Moslem and Hindu worlds. We have a huge job to do, and we don't dare let this opportunity pass us by. If ever there was a time for God's people to rally and put their shoulders to the wheel, it is now. We must come alive through the Holy Spirit and supply the effort and the money to get the job done. The time is at hand for a major victory.

5

That My House May Be Filled

GOD IS HAVING HIS WAY!

He is creating opportunities for a great spiritual awakening, which I believe is underway.

I call your attention to Luke 14:15-23.

> And when one of them that sat at meat with him heard these things, he said unto him, Blessed is he that shall eat bread in the kingdom of God. Then said he unto him, A certain man made a great supper, and bade many: And sent his servant at supper time to say to them that were bidden, Come; for all things are now ready.
>
> And they all with one consent began to make excuse. The first said unto him, I have bought a piece of ground, and I must needs go and see it: I pray thee have me excused. And another said, I have bought five yoke of oxen, and I go to prove them: I pray thee have me excused. And another said, I have married a wife, and therefore I cannot come.
>
> So that servant came, and shewed his lord these things. Then the master of the house being angry said to his servant, Go out quickly into the streets and lanes of the city, and bring in hither the poor, and the maimed, and the halt, and the blind. And the servant said, Lord, it is done as thou hast commanded, and yet there is room. And the lord said unto the servant, Go out into the highways and hedges, and compel them to come in, that my house may be filled.

In this passage of Scripture, we have the parable of the great supper. The master sent his servant out to bid

55

everyone to come to the supper. The first group made all sorts of ridiculous excuses why they couldn't come.

Notice how ridiculous they were. Who would buy a piece of land without first looking at it? Who would buy oxen (which would be like buying a tractor, car, or truck, today) without examining them first? These people gave lame excuses and said, "We can't come." Another said, "I've married a wife and I can't come." That's a poor excuse for a man not to go to the house of God.

So the master sent the servant out the second time and said, **Go into the streets and lanes of the city and bring in hither the poor, and the maimed, and the halt and the blind.** The servant came back very quickly and said, **It is done as thou hast commanded. Then he said, Go out into the highways and hedges, and compel them to come in, that my house may be filled.**

The only compelling power the Church has is the power of the Holy Spirit operating in love. The Holy Spirit works in love, the greatest and most powerful emotion of all. So the master says to his servant, "Go in the power of the Holy Spirit and the love of God and compel men and women to come into my house that it may be full." When God says His house is going to be full, it's going to be full.

It will take a numberless multitude of people to fill God's house — just a few hundred million will not fill His house. Revelation 21 and 22 speak of the New Jerusalem, a city 1,500 miles square. This is the Father's house. He will reside there.

The Holy Spirit will accomplish His assignment. His earthly outpouring, which began in Jerusalem ten days after Jesus ascended to heaven, is to continue throughout the last days, which includes the seven years of Tribulation (see Joel 2:28-31).

Paul prophesies in Ephesians 4:11-16 about the Church becoming mature, growing into a perfect man like Jesus, and beginning to increase — not decrease.

And He gave some, apostles; and some, prophets; and some, evangelists; and some, pastors and teachers; for the perfecting of the saints, for the work of the ministry, for the edifying of the body of Christ: Till we all come in the unity of the faith, and of the knowledge of the Son of God, unto a perfect man, unto the measure of the stature of the fulness of Christ:

That we henceforth be no more children, tossed to and fro, and carried about with every wind of doctrine, by the sleight of men, and cunning craftiness, whereby they lie in wait to deceive; but speaking the truth in love, may grow up into him in all things, which is the head, even Christ:

From whom the whole body fitly joined together and compacted by that which every joint supplieth, according to the effectual working in the measure of every part, maketh increase of the body unto the edifying of itself in love.

The prophecies of Isaiah, chapter 2, and Micah, chapter 4, agree with Joel 2:28-31. What beautiful harmony of Bible truth, which Paul confirms throughout his epistles.

We are on the threshold of a mighty, worldwide spiritual awakening and revival. The Church will come into new spiritual heights of holiness, dedication, commitment, and discipline. It's going to be dynamic and it will sweep the entire world! Doors cannot be closed on God — Satan cannot shut God out.

Occasionally, one may hear that doors are being closed to the Gospel. Doors may be closed to certain people or ministries, but they are not closed to God. You cannot shut Him out. You cannot close the door on Him. If a nation or government tries to do so, God will open other doors and move in from a different direction.

The plan of God for the salvation of mankind must be carried out. Romans 10:13,14 gives magnificent insight as to how it is being done. **For whosoever shall call upon the name of the Lord shall be saved. How then shall they call on him in whom they have not believed? And how shall they believe in Him of whom they have not heard? And how shall they hear without a preacher?** Remember, there are more than two billion people in the Soviet Union, Eastern European nations, and the Orient who, for decades, have had little opportunity to call upon the name of the Lord.

> **How then shall they call on Him in whom they have not believed? and how shall they believe in him of whom they have not heard? and how shall they hear without a preacher? And how shall they preach, except they be sent? as it is written, How beautiful are the feet of them that preach the gospel of peace, and bring glad tidings of good things!**
>
> **Romans 10:14,15**

It's Time For the Harvest

The time has come for the masses of people who have been oppressed, harassed, imprisoned, and restrained to hear the good news. Romans 10:17 says, **So then faith cometh by hearing, and hearing by the Word of God.**

God is not going to supernaturally sweep over these masses of people and cause them to have dreams and wake up saying, "Oh, I dreamed about a Savior and now I accept Him." It is not going to happen that way.

Masses of people will accept Jesus because He has been lovingly preached to them in the anointing and power of the Holy Spirit. Remember, the Scripture declares that it is **not by might, nor by power, but by my spirit, saith the Lord of hosts** (Zech. 4:6). God will reach all mankind by using His tried-and-proven plan.

Thank God, the Soviets under Lenin, Stalin, Khrushchev, and Brezhnev did not kill all the Christians in the Soviet Union. Christians have managed to survive and now they are increasing in large numbers. Christianity will soon sweep the Soviet Union in a tidal wave.

In spite of all the efforts of the Chinese communists to kill all the Christians in China, they failed. It is estimated that there are approximately 50 million born-again Christians in China who know Jesus Christ.

The one billion people in China need our prayerful support. Soon the Bamboo Curtain will open and God-called men must be ready to step in and spread the Gospel across this vast land.

Be careful not to create your own call to this task (be God-called, not self-called) and don't be influenced by others. If God's work is to be accomplished in this mighty mission field, it will be through those He has chosen and prepared for the task — those who stand ready to carry the message into this area when the door is opened.

It is God's will that the Word be preached in all the world. The preaching of the Word will bring faith and, because of that faith, the masses of lost souls will come into the kingdom of God. GOD IS HAVING HIS WAY!

Will There Be a "Falling Away"?

Occasionally someone points out 2 Thessalonians 2, which reveals a falling away before the day when Jesus returns to reign. The Apostle Paul does make that statement in 2 Thessalonians 2:3, **Let no man deceive you by any means: for that day shall not come, except there come a falling away first, and that man of sin be revealed, the son of perdition.** He speaks of a falling away. Some, however, cannot accept that a great harvest could coincide with the "falling away."

One cannot fall away from something that does not exist. The Word of God indicates there is a mighty outpouring of the Holy Spirit sweeping multitudes into the Kingdom while others, who have been in the Kingdom, are falling away. In 1 Timothy 4:1, Paul writes, **Now the Spirit speaketh expressly, that in the latter times some shall depart from the faith, giving heed to seducing spirits, and doctrines of devils.**

I recently ministered in Europe and Africa and I can tell you that the spiritual awakening has very definitely begun. There is no question about it — it's developing in a very powerful way, step by step. God is having His way and He will not allow anyone to hinder His handiwork.

However, we cannot deny that there will be a falling away. Men and women will depart from the faith and give themselves over to seducing, deceiving spirits and doctrines of devils. As a matter of fact, it is happening right here in our nation at this present time. There are many strange doctrines being propagated among the saints.

Paul prophesied both — the falling away and the mature, increasing Church (see Eph. 4:11-16). Paul also prophesied that the Church would be caught up by Jesus, that he might present it to himself a glorious church, not having spot, or wrinkle, or any such thing; but that it should be holy and without blemish (Eph. 5:27). Some teach that the Church will not be glorious until Jesus comes and takes it to himself. But the biblical reason He receives the Church is because it is gloriously, spiritually mature.

What, then, should we, as Christians, do? John says, **Beloved, now are we the sons of God, and it doth not yet appear what we shall be: but we know that, when he shall appear, we shall be like him; for we shall see him as he is. And every man that hath this hope in him purifieth himself, even as he is pure** (1 John 3:2,3). In order to meet

Jesus in the air, you must be ready — pure. There's no middle ground. Ready or not, He's coming for His Church.

What Will We Do?

Many "Christians" continue to sit around warming the pew, finding fault, complaining, arguing with one another, and changing churches every few years because they don't want to be committed. But, saints of God, the fields are white unto harvest, the Holy Ghost is mightily at work, and God is having His way! And it's time to grow up and become the purified people of God, reaching out to a lost world.

Christians must crucify the flesh and its carnal desires, put aside the weights and cares of life, repent of sin, and subject their thoughts to Jesus Christ. If you intend to defeat Satan, win souls, live victoriously, and be ready to meet Jesus in the air, you will purify yourself and learn obedience.

Since it is so evident that God is having His way among the nations, the Church must allow Him to also have His way with them. God's Word is the bottom line and He will have the last word. The Word is simple, plain, and easily understood. You say, "Hilton, you can say that because you've studied it your entire life and have preached it for forty years." Well, God is no respecter of persons. He loves you and His Word was written so you could understand it and use it as a guide for your life.

We need to learn obedience to the Word, which simply means we're no longer going to allow our flesh to control us. Allow the Spirit-man to prevail and the flesh will receive understanding and learn obedience and get in line with the Word of God and the Holy Spirit. As we mature, we find it is easier to be in agreement with the men God has set among us.

Paul instructs us to know those who labor among us and are over us in the Lord. That's good instruction. You should know that you are following an anointed man of God. The Holy Spirit can show you his fruits and give you a peaceful inner witness. The Holy Spirit can lead, guide, and direct you, and much of this guidance comes through anointed ministries of good report. Paul says, Let no one deceive you by any means. Never follow a preacher because of his personality, his great speaking ability, his large following, or even because there are some signs and wonders. Become part of a congregation where the Holy Spirit has total freedom and liberty all the time. Put your roots down and stay there. Become disciplined and take part in the operation. Get in harmony with the spiritual leadership and you will discover how easy it is to obey God and the leadership of the Holy Spirit. Let God have the last word. Allow His Word to be the bottom line in your life.

Get Involved in the Harvest

Are there any further recommendations? Yes. We are to become involved with the harvest.

Say not ye, There are yet four months, and then cometh harvest? behold, I say unto you, Lift up your eyes, and look on the fields; for they are white already to harvest (John 4:35). Friends, the fields are white — it's time to work in the harvest.

We are spiritually born again to be soul winners. There is no such thing as a man or woman being a follower of Jesus and not winning souls. First, we should purify ourselves. Then we should become obedient to our Heavenly Father and His Word through the Holy Spirit. At this point we should become involved in the harvest, based on John 4:35 and Matthew 4:19.

In Matthew 4:19, Jesus is speaking to His disciples. We are also His followers and disciples and He speaks to every one of us when He says Follow me, and I will make you fishers of men. To follow Jesus Christ is to be a soul winner.

When we follow Jesus, He makes us fishers of men and we have a guaranteed catch. Every born-again child of God is enabled by the Holy Spirit to win someone else to Jesus. Every believer should be about the business of winning someone to Jesus Christ — at home and abroad.

Let's not focus our eyes on the foreign harvest and miss the opportunities in our own back yard. Jesus said to His followers in Acts 1:8, **But ye shall receive power, after that the Holy Ghost is come upon you: and ye shall be witnesses unto me both in Jerusalem, and in all Judea, and in Samaria, and unto the uttermost part of the earth. You will receive power to be His witness and representative.** Where did He say you should witness? In Jerusalem — that's your own neighborhood. And in Judea — that's the county in which you live. And in Samaria — that's the state in which you live. And in the uttermost parts of the earth. So start winning souls right where you are. Then, if God chooses to send you to the foreign harvest fields, you will be ready.

Look for Christ's Appearing

What else shall we do, now that these tremendous prophecies are being fulfilled? We are to look for Jesus in His glorious appearing. When it happens, He's going to shout, ''Come up here!'' and we're going to be caught up to meet Him in the air. Then we will proceed with Him to the Throne of God as conquering heroes. The army of God will have arrived from earth to stand victorious with Jesus before the throne.

Jesus tells us to look for His appearing. In Luke 21:28, He said, **And when these things begin to come to pass, then look up, and lift up your heads; for your redemption draweth nigh.** What things? The things He prophesied in the previous verses — the repossession of the city of Jerusalem, which was fulfilled in 1967, the space program, manmade signs in the heavens, distress of nations with perplexity, which has been fulfilled by the massive upheaval of people in every nation — lawlessness. When these things begin to come to pass, then look up, and lift up your heads; for your redemption draweth nigh. The word "look" used by Jesus means, "to eagerly anticipate the event with joyous preparation."

Jesus is clearly saying that when these prophecies — the prophecies we have discussed in this book — begin to be fulfilled, it is time for the Church to look up in eager anticipation of His appearing with joyous preparation. There is no more joyous preparation than to be about the Master's business — winning souls, seeing people healed, delivered, and set free.

We should be anxious to gather in the house of God as we see prophecies being fulfilled that tell us Jesus is coming soon! There, we bring the new believers we have won and together worship and praise our Savior. Look up, and lift up your heads; for your redemption draweth nigh.

Glorification of the physical body is the last phase of salvation. Paul picks up this truth in Titus 2:13, **Looking for that blessed hope, and the glorious appearing of the great God and our Saviour Jesus Christ.** Paul instructs us to be looking for — or continuing to eagerly anticipate — Christ's appearing.

> **Teaching us that, denying ungodliness and worldly lusts, we should live soberly, righteously, and godly, in this present world; Looking for that blessed hope, and the glorious appearing of the great God and our Savior Jesus Christ. Who gave Himself for us, that He might redeem us from all iniquity, and purify unto himself a peculiar people, zealous of good works.**
>
> **Titus 2:12-14**

Paul continues in Hebrews 9:28, **So Christ was once offered to bear the sins of many; and unto them that look for Him shall He appear the second time without sin unto salvation.** To those who look for Him, He will appear a second time. The first appearing was not His first coming, which was as a baby, born to the Virgin Mary, in Bethlehem of Judea, as prophesied by the Prophet Isaiah. His first appearing followed His glorious Resurrection when He appeared to Mary. His second appearing will be as Paul describes it in First Thessalonians 4:16-18, when He appears in the skies and shouts, "Come up here," as He did to John in Revelation 4:1:

> After this I looked, and, behold, a door was opened in heaven: and the first voice which I heard was as it were of a trumpet talking with me; which said, Come up hither, and I will shew thee things which must be hereafter.

When Jesus shouts, "Come up here," only the dead in Christ and the Christians who are looking for Him will hear His voice. They will be caught up in the air to meet the Lord and instantly their physical bodies will be glorified and they will proceed with Christ to the Throne of God. Those who are caught up will be the ones who were in the harvest fields, about the Master's business (see Matt. 24:44-47).

The event of Christ's appearing is not to be confused with His glorious return to the earth. When He returns to the earth to reign, He returns according to Zechariah 14:5: **And ye shall flee to the valley of the mountains; for the valley of the mountains shall reach unto Azal: yea, ye shall flee, like as ye fled from before the earthquake in the days of Uzziah king of Judah: and the Lord my God shall come, and all the saints with thee.** Revelation 17:14: **These shall make war with the Lamb, and the Lamb shall overcome them: for He is Lord of lords, and King of kings: and they that are with Him are called, and chosen, and faithful.** And Revelation 19:14: **And the armies which were in heaven followed him upon white horses, clothed in fine linen, white and clean.** The saints, His army, come back with Him, from heaven to earth. On that occasion, He has to deal with the wicked and ungodly one more time at the Battle of Armageddon.

So, at His appearing, He has only to receive the Church unto Himself. We should be looking for Him and make ready for that event.

Be Ready!

In Matthew 24:44, Jesus said, **Therefore be ye also ready: for in such an hour as ye think not the Son of man cometh.** Throughout the Gospels and the teachings of Paul, we are admonished to be ready. Get ready. Be prayed up and filled with the Holy Ghost and operate on the Word of God. Remember, you cannot pastor yourself. You need to be part of a spiritually alive, sound congregation. Put down roots, produce much fruit on your spiritual tree, and win souls. Don't be a maverick; don't free-lance. Be part of what God is doing through His Body. Shun the identity of a "rebel." Rebellion is as the sin of witchcraft (see 1 Sam. 15:23).

God doesn't need any superstars. If you think that's what you're going to become, you will run squarely into situations you cannot handle. And it won't be God's fault. So, it's time for God's people to get ready and stay that way. You get ready by walking with the Lord Jesus Christ daily, 365 days every year.

And he said to them all, If any man will come after me, let him deny himself, and take up his cross daily, and follow me (Luke 9:23). Following Jesus is a full-time job. It means more than just attending a Sunday and mid-week service. Follow Him daily — every day — in your home, in your neighborhood, in your work place, or where you are doing business.

We must be ready for His appearing. Matthew 25:1-10 reveals the story of the ten virgins.

Then shall the kingdom of heaven be likened unto ten virgins, which took their lamps, and went forth to meet the bridegroom. And five of them were wise, and five were foolish. They that were foolish took their lamps, and took no oil with them: But the wise took oil in their vessels with their lamps. While the bridegroom tarried, they all slumbered and slept.

And at midnight there was a cry made, Behold, the bridegroom cometh; go ye out to meet him. Then all those virgins arose, and trimmed their lamps. And the foolish said unto the wise, Give us of your oil; for our lamps are gone out. But the wise answered, saying, Not so; lest there be not enough for us and you: but go ye rather to them that sell, and buy for yourselves.

And while they went to buy, the bridegroom came; and they that were ready went in with him to the marriage: and the door was shut.

The wise ones were the ones who were ready for the event which was about to take place. What event? The bridegroom was about to appear, and when he did, only those who were ready went into the wedding chamber with him.

The foolish virgins were not ready. They did not go into the wedding chamber, which is symbolic of the catching up of the saints. MAKE CERTAIN YOU ARE READY!

The dismantling of the Soviet Union and its maneuvering for a greater role in Middle Eastern affairs is, without question, fulfilling Ezekial 38. Coinciding with this is the strong quest for peace between Israel and its Arab neighbors. These events could happen very quickly or take some time. Once peace exists in the Middle East, the stage will be set for a Soviet move on Israel — and as we have seen, this means the total destruction of the Soviet Empire.

Afterword

Yes, events in the last two years have, indeed, been dynamic, momentous and unusual. "Change" has been the order of the day. I do believe that God is using these events and changes to get attention. Whose attention? Yours. Mine. The Church's.

Why? God is having His way. His plan as outlined in the Bible is unfolding before us. We are each part of that plan and He wants our part to be an active one. As I mentioned earlier, He wants us in His army, aware of our rank, our position, and reporting for duty. If you haven't already "enlisted," it is easy to do. He tells us how in Romans 10:9,10,13. He doesn't care where you are or who you are, or what you have done. He says so in Ephesians 2:1-8. Whoever you are, whoever you have been, God has a position and assignment for you in His Church, in His army.

Enlist now. It's as easy as this:

Heavenly Father, according to Your Word, I believe in my heart that You raised Your Son, Jesus, from the dead. I accept Jesus Christ as my Lord and Savior. I claim and receive Your grace and my salvation right now. Thank You, Father, in Jesus' Name, Amen.

Welcome, brother or sister. Welcome to the fellowship — the army — the Church of our Lord.

The pace of events and changes is accelerating. More and more people (literally billions around the world) can now, or soon will be able to, hear and receive God's Word — if only they have someone to hear it from! You guessed it. That is your first and continuing assignment in God's forces, just as it is every Christian's.

But, just as any earthly commander would not expect his troops to accomplish a mission without the necessary equipment, God, too, wants you properly equipped — with power — with the power of the Holy Spirit as explained in Acts 1:8. Ask Him to issue it to you now.

Lord, I come in the name of Jesus Christ, asking to be filled with the power of the Holy Spirit so that I may be a witness for the Lord Jesus Christ. In Jesus' name, Amen.

Bibliography

Information on the fifteen Soviet Republics and nations under control of the Soviet Union, including dates of events affecting the Soviet republics, Eastern European nations, and China came from the *World Book*.

Figures for the population of the Soviet Union, Eastern European nations, other European nations affected and controlled by communism, China, and other Oriental nations affected and controlled by communism were taken from the 1989 volume of the *World Almanac*.

Hilton Sutton is regarded by many people as the nation's foremost authority on Bible prophecy as related to current events and world affairs.

As an ordained minister of the Gospel, Dr. Sutton served as pastor for several years before entering his present prophetic assignment. Today he travels throughout the world, teaching and preaching God's Word. He takes the words of the most accurate news report ever — the Word of God — and relates it to the news today.

Having spent over twenty years researching and studying the book of Revelation, Hilton Sutton explains Bible prophecy and world affairs to the people in a way that is clear, concise and easy to understand. He presents his messages on a layman's level and shows the Bible to be the most accurate, up-to-date book ever written.

Hilton Sutton and his family make their home in Humble, Texas, where he serves as chairman of the board of Mission to America, a Christian organization dedicated to carrying the Gospel of Jesus Christ to the world.

To receive Hilton Sutton's
monthly publication, *Update*,
write:

Mission to America
Hilton Sutton Ministries
736 Wilson Road
Humble, Texas 77338

*Please include your prayer requests
and comments when you write.*

Other Books by Hilton Sutton

Revelation — God's Grand Finale

Revelation Syllabus
Companion Study Guide to *Revelation*

Familiar Spirits, Witchcraft and Satanism
Innocent Beginnings, Deadly Results

Pre-Tribulation Rapture of the Church

U.S. in Prophetic Events

Rapture — Ready or Not

**Available from your local bookstore,
or from:**

Harrison House
P. O. Box 35035
Tulsa, OK 74153

Emma Savarese
29 Tenafly Dr
new Hyde Park   NY

Whatever the need of the moment, the answer is to be found in Scripture, if we take the time to search for it. Whatever we're feeling, whatever we're suffering, whatever we're hoping—the Bible has something to say to us.

This collection of Bible verses is meant for use as a handy reference when you feel the need for the Bible's guidance on a particular problem in your life. It is in no way intended to replace regular Bible study or the use of a concordance for in-depth study of a subject. There are many facets of your life—and many topics in the Bible—that are not covered here.

But if you are feeling extremely lonely one day, some of the Bible's wisdom and comfort is available to you here under the topic of Loneliness. All topics are arranged alphabetically, for ease of use.

All Scripture is from The King James Version of the Bible.

Tel 741 6261

The Bible Promise Book

Barbour and Company, Inc.
164 Mill Street
Westwood, New Jersey

©1985 by Barbour and Company, Inc.

All rights reserved. No part of this publication may be reproduced or transmitted in any form or by any means without written permission of the publisher.

Leatherette Edition ISBN 0-916441-43-1
Bonded Leather Edition ISBN 0-916441-44-X
Bonded Leather Flexible Edition ISBN 1-55748-039-7

Published by: **BARBOUR AND COMPANY, INC.**
                164 Mill Street
                Westwood, New Jersey 07675

            (In Canada, THE CHRISTIAN LIBRARY,
         960 The Gateway, Burlington, Ontario L7L 5K7)

EVANGELICAL CHRISTIAN PUBLISHERS ASSOCIATION **ecpa** MEMBER

Printed in the United States of America

Contents

In Canada contact:

Word Alive
P. O. Box 284
Niverville, Manitoba
CANADA R0A 1EO

For international sales in Europe,
contact:

Harrison House Europe
Belruptstrasse 42 A
A — 6900 Bregenz
AUSTRIA

The Harrison House Vision

Proclaiming the truth and the power
Of the Gospel of Jesus Christ
With excellence;

Challenging Christians to
Live victoriously,
Grow spiritually,
Know God Intimately.